The Healing of Internal Self

Rodny Lamarre

CIP data on file with the National Library and Archives

Print edition: ISBN 978-1-55483-538-6
E-book edition: ISBN 978-1-55483-539-3

Contents

Introduction

In a world filled with constant distractions and external pressures, we often neglect the most crucial aspect of our existence: our internal self. "The Healing of Internal Self" takes you on a transformative journey towards self-discovery, healing, and personal growth. Drawing upon ancient wisdom, psychological insights, and practical exercises, this book serves as a guide to navigate the intricate landscapes of your inner world.

The human experience is fraught with challenges, pain, and emotional scars. Within the pages of this book, you will embark on a profound exploration of your inner turmoil, unmasking the hidden wounds that have shaped your life. Through self-reflection and the power of self-compassion, you will learn to illuminate the shadows that cloud your true essence.

Each chapter offers detailed information, insightful anecdotes, and actionable steps to facilitate your healing process. You will delve into the depths of vulnerability, shedding societal masks to reveal your authentic self. By breaking patterns and releasing emotional baggage, you will forge a path towards liberation and personal freedom.

This book emphasizes the importance of nurturing resilience and embracing your unique journey. You will discover how to cultivate meaningful relationships and connect deeply with others, creating a support network that nurtures and uplifts. Through the exploration of creativity, you will learn to express your inner voice and find solace in the transformative power of art.

"The Healing of Internal Self" also delves into the profound impact of forgiveness, guiding you towards liberating your heart from the shackles of resentment. As you embrace change and learn to thrive in transformation, you will cultivate gratitude and open the doors to abundant possibilities.

Join us on this extraordinary odyssey of self-discovery, where the healing of your internal self paves the way for a life lived to its fullest potential. Are you ready to embark on this transformative journey?

Chapter 1

Acknowledging the Wounds
The Path to Healing Begins

In Chapter 1, "Acknowledging the Wounds: The Path to Healing Begins," we explore the importance of recognizing and acknowledging our internal wounds as the initial step towards healing. We delve into the profound impact that unaddressed emotional pain can have on our well-being and provide guidance on how to bravely confront and embrace our wounds.

We begin by discussing the significance of self-awareness and introspection. By turning our attention inward, we can identify and understand the wounds that reside within us. We explore various forms of emotional pain, such as past traumas, unresolved conflicts, and negative self-beliefs, and emphasize the importance of acknowledging their presence in our lives.

Next, we delve into the emotional journey of

facing our wounds. We explore the range of emotions that may arise, including fear, sadness, anger, and vulnerability. Through compassionate self-reflection and gentle self-care, we create a safe and supportive space to navigate this challenging terrain.

Furthermore, we discuss the power of self-compassion in the healing process. We encourage readers to extend kindness and understanding to themselves as they explore their wounds. By practicing self-compassion, we create a nurturing environment that allows healing to unfold at its own pace.

In addition, we explore the significance of seeking support during this journey. Whether it be through therapy, support groups, or trusted friends and family, we emphasize the value of having a compassionate and non-judgmental presence to lean on. Through shared experiences and guidance, we can find solace, validation, and encouragement as we navigate our healing journey.

Throughout this chapter, we provide reflective exercises and practical tools to support readers in acknowledging and embracing their wounds. By taking this crucial first step, we open the door to profound personal transformation and the potential for deep healing.

Chapter 2

Unearthing the Roots
Exploring the Source of Internal Pain

In Chapter 2, "Unearthing the Roots: Exploring the Source of Internal Pain," we delve into the process of uncovering the underlying causes and roots of our internal pain. We recognize that healing requires an understanding of the origins of our wounds and provide guidance on exploring and addressing these sources.

We begin by emphasizing the importance of self-reflection and curiosity. By gently delving into our past experiences, relationships, and patterns of behavior, we can begin to identify the events or circumstances that have contributed to our internal pain. We encourage readers to approach this exploration with openness and a willingness to uncover hidden truths.

Next, we explore the impact of childhood experiences on our internal landscape. We delve into the influence of family dynamics, early traumas, and attachment styles on our emotional well-being. Through this exploration, we can gain insight into how these experiences have shaped our beliefs, behaviors, and relationships.

Furthermore, we discuss the significance of self-forgiveness and compassion as we uncover the roots of our pain. By understanding that our past experiences were shaped by a variety of factors, including external circumstances and the limitations of those around us, we can cultivate self-compassion and release self-blame.

In addition, we explore the role of journaling and expressive writing in the process of unearthing the roots of our pain. By engaging in these practices, we create a safe space for self-expression, introspection, and emotional release. Through writing, we can gain clarity and insights into our experiences, facilitating the healing process.

Throughout this chapter, we provide journal prompts and reflection exercises to support readers in unearthing the roots of their internal pain. By bravely exploring the sources of our wounds, we lay the foundation for profound healing and personal growth.

Chapter 3

Nurturing Self-Compassion
Embracing Kindness and
Understanding

In Chapter 3, "Nurturing Self-Compassion: Embracing Kindness and Understanding," we delve into the power of self-compassion as a vital aspect of the healing journey. We explore the transformative effects of extending kindness, understanding, and acceptance to ourselves and provide guidance on cultivating a nurturing relationship with our inner selves.

We begin by defining self-compassion as the practice of treating ourselves with the same care and compassion we would offer to a loved one. We discuss the three core components of self-compassion: self-kindness, common humanity, and mindfulness. By embracing these elements, we create a foundation for deep self-healing.

Next, we explore the role of self-talk in cultivating self-compassion. We delve into the impact of our inner dialogue and provide strategies for shifting self-criticism into self-encouragement and understanding. Through mindfulness and awareness, we can challenge negative self-talk and cultivate a more compassionate and supportive inner voice.

Furthermore, we discuss the importance of self-care in nurturing self-compassion. We explore practices such as mindfulness meditation, self-reflection, and engaging in activities that bring joy and nourishment. By prioritizing our well-being and practicing self-care, we create a nurturing environment for self-compassion to flourish.

In addition, we delve into the concept of self-forgiveness and its role in the healing process. We explore the benefits of releasing self-blame and guilt, allowing ourselves to heal and move forward with greater compassion and acceptance. Through forgiveness, we free ourselves from the burdens of the past and create space for deep healing.

Throughout this chapter, we provide practical exercises and self-reflective prompts to support readers in nurturing self-compassion. By embracing kindness, understanding, and acceptance towards ourselves, we foster an environment of healing, growth, and unconditional love.

Chapter 4

Cultivating Emotional Resilience
Building Inner Strength

In Chapter 4, "Cultivating Emotional Resilience: Building Inner Strength," we explore the concept of emotional resilience and its significance in the healing process. We delve into the skills and practices that help us navigate challenging emotions, setbacks, and adversity, fostering inner strength and growth.

We begin by defining emotional resilience as the ability to adapt and bounce back from difficulties and emotional hardships. We discuss the importance of recognizing and embracing a wide range of emotions, allowing ourselves to experience them fully while maintaining a sense of inner stability.

Next, we explore the role of self-awareness in cultivating emotional resilience. We discuss the importance of understanding our emotional triggers, patterns, and responses. Through self-reflection and mindfulness, we can develop a deeper understanding of our emotional landscape and build the capacity to respond to challenges in a more resilient manner.

Furthermore, we delve into the practice of self-regulation and emotional self-care. We explore techniques such as deep breathing, grounding exercises, and stress management strategies that help us navigate intense emotions and maintain emotional balance. By nurturing our emotional well-being, we cultivate the inner strength needed to face and overcome adversity.

In addition, we discuss the significance of fostering supportive relationships and seeking external support. We emphasize the value of connecting with trusted individuals who can provide guidance, validation, and encouragement. Through these connections, we create a network of support that contributes to our emotional resilience.

Throughout this chapter, we provide practical exercises and tools to support readers in cultivating emotional resilience. By developing the skills to navigate challenging emotions and setbacks, we build inner strength and create a foundation for sustainable healing and personal growth.

Chapter 5

The Power of Self-Reflection
Gaining Insights and Clarity

In Chapter 5, "The Power of Self-Reflection: Gaining Insights and Clarity," we explore the transformative effects of self-reflection in the healing process. We delve into the practice of introspection and provide guidance on gaining insights, clarity, and self-understanding.

We begin by discussing the significance of creating dedicated time and space for self-reflection. We emphasize the importance of setting aside moments of solitude and silence to connect with our inner selves. Through self-reflection, we create an opportunity to pause, listen to our inner voice, and gain deeper insights into our thoughts, feelings, and experiences.

Next, we explore various tools and practices that facilitate self-reflection. We discuss journaling, meditation, mindfulness, and other contemplative exercises as means of exploring our inner landscape. By engaging in these practices, we create a channel for self-expression, introspection, and the discovery of profound truths about ourselves.

Furthermore, we delve into the process of gaining insights and clarity through self-reflection. We explore the questions and prompts that can guide us in uncovering hidden beliefs, patterns, and desires. Through self-inquiry and honest introspection, we create a foundation for self-awareness and personal transformation.

In addition, we discuss the role of self-compassion in self-reflection. We emphasize the importance of approaching self-reflection with kindness, curiosity, and non-judgment. By cultivating self-compassion, we create a safe and supportive environment for exploring our inner landscape without fear or self-criticism.

Throughout this chapter, we provide practical exercises and reflection prompts to support readers in engaging in self-reflection. By gaining insights and clarity about ourselves, our experiences, and our desires, we open the doors to profound self-discovery, healing, and growth.

Chapter 6

The Art of Letting Go
Releasing Emotional Baggage

In this chapter, we delve into the profound process of letting go and releasing the emotional baggage that weighs us down. We explore the various aspects of our lives where we may be holding on to past hurts, regrets, and negative experiences. Through introspection and self-reflection, we uncover the root causes of our attachments and discover the freedom that comes with letting go.

One of the fundamental principles we discuss is acceptance—the acceptance of what has been and what cannot be changed. We explore the art of forgiveness, not only towards others but also towards ourselves. We understand that holding on to resentment and anger only serves to imprison us in our own suffering. Through forgiveness, we liberate ourselves from the chains of the past and create space for healing and growth.

We also explore the power of gratitude as a transformative tool in the process of letting go. By shifting our focus from what we have lost or what has hurt us to the abundance and blessings present in our lives, we open ourselves up to new possibilities and experiences. Gratitude allows us to cultivate a sense of peace and contentment in the present moment, enhancing our ability to release what no longer serves us.

Furthermore, we discuss the importance of self-compassion in the journey of letting go. We often carry guilt and self-blame for past mistakes or perceived failures. Through self-compassion, we learn to extend kindness, understanding, and forgiveness to ourselves. This practice empowers us to release the burden of self-judgment and embrace our inherent worthiness.

Throughout this chapter, we provide practical exercises and techniques to facilitate the process of letting go. From journaling and meditation to rituals and symbolic acts, we offer a range of tools to support you on your path toward emotional liberation. By actively engaging in these practices, you will develop the resilience and strength needed to release emotional baggage and embrace a lighter, more fulfilling existence.

Remember, letting go is not a one-time event but an ongoing practice. As we continue to grow and evolve, new layers of attachment may emerge. This chapter equips you with the understanding and tools to navigate these challenges, allowing you to experience the true freedom that comes from releasing emotional baggage.

Chapter 7

Cultivating Resilience
Building Inner Strength

In this chapter, we explore the concept of resilience and its profound impact on our ability to navigate life's challenges with grace and strength. Resilience is not an innate trait but a skill that can be cultivated and developed over time. By understanding the core elements of resilience and implementing practical strategies, you can build inner strength and embrace the adversities of life as opportunities for growth.

We begin by examining the mindset of resilience—an optimistic and growth-oriented perspective that views setbacks as temporary and surmountable. We explore the power of reframing negative experiences and shifting our focus to the lessons and strengths that emerge from adversity. By adopting a resilient mindset, we become better equipped to face challenges head-on and persevere through difficult times.

Next, we delve into the importance of self-care in nurturing resilience. We explore various dimensions of self-care, including physical, emotional, and mental well-being. From establishing healthy routines and prioritizing rest to engaging in activities that bring joy and nourishment, we provide practical tips to help you create a self-care practice that supports your resilience.

We also discuss the significance of cultivating a strong support network. Human connection is a vital component of resilience, and fostering meaningful relationships can provide us with the emotional support and encouragement needed during challenging times. We delve into effective communication, setting boundaries, and seeking support when necessary, empowering you to build a resilient network of individuals who uplift and inspire you.

Furthermore, we explore the role of self-belief and self-efficacy in resilience. By recognizing your strengths, acknowledging your past successes, and cultivating a sense of self-worth, you enhance your ability to face adversity with confidence. We provide practical exercises and techniques to develop self-belief and overcome self-doubt, enabling you to build inner resilience.

Throughout this chapter, we emphasize the importance of embracing flexibility and adaptability. Life is unpredictable, and resilience allows us to adjust our sails and navigate the storms. By cultivating a mindset of flexibility and embracing change, you become more adept at bouncing back from setbacks and finding new opportunities for growth and fulfillment.

Remember, resilience is not about avoiding or denying pain but about developing the strength and skills to overcome it. By embracing the principles and practices discussed in this chapter, you can build inner resilience, transforming challenges into catalysts for personal growth and flourishing.

Chapter 8

Awakening Authenticity
Embracing Your True Self

In this chapter, we embark on a journey of self-discovery and explore the concept of authenticity. We delve into the masks we wear and the societal expectations that often lead us astray from our true selves. By understanding the importance of authenticity and embracing our unique identities, we open ourselves up to a life of purpose, fulfillment, and genuine connections.

We begin by examining the societal pressures and conditioning that can mask our authentic selves. From childhood influences to cultural norms, we unravel the layers that may have obscured our true essence. By acknowledging these influences, we empower ourselves to challenge and transcend societal expectations, embracing the path of authenticity.

Next, we delve into self-awareness as a key

component of embracing authenticity. Through introspection, reflection, and self-exploration, we gain a deeper understanding of our values, passions, and desires. By aligning our thoughts, actions, and choices with our authentic selves, we cultivate a sense of congruence and integrity.

Furthermore, we explore the courage it takes to be authentic in a world that often encourages conformity. We delve into the fears and insecurities that may arise when stepping into our true selves, and we provide practical strategies to overcome these obstacles. By embracing vulnerability and cultivating self-acceptance, we unlock the power of authenticity and invite others to do the same.

Throughout this chapter, we offer exercises, prompts, and reflections to guide you on your journey towards authenticity. From journaling and self-expression to exploring your passions and reconnecting with your inner child, we provide tools to help you embrace and celebrate your unique essence.

Remember, authenticity is a lifelong pursuit. It requires continuous self-discovery, self-compassion, and the willingness to show up as your true self, even when faced with challenges. By embracing authenticity, you invite others to do the same and create a ripple effect of genuine connections and meaningful relationships.

Chapter 9

Connecting with Others
Creating Meaningful Relationships

In this chapter, we delve into the profound significance of human connection and explore the art of creating meaningful relationships. We recognize that authentic connections are essential for our well-being and growth, and by cultivating meaningful relationships, we enrich our lives and the lives of others.

We begin by exploring the foundations of healthy relationships—trust, respect, and effective communication. We delve into the importance of active listening, empathy, and understanding in fostering deep connections. By developing these skills, we create a safe space for open and honest communication, where genuine connections can flourish.

Next, we examine the power of vulnerability in building meaningful relationships. We embrace the courage to share our authentic selves, including our hopes, dreams, fears, and vulnerabilities. By opening up and allowing others to see us as we truly are, we create a space for intimacy and connection that transcends surface-level interactions.

Furthermore, we discuss the significance of boundaries in relationships. Boundaries allow us to honor our needs, values, and personal space while maintaining healthy dynamics with others. We delve into the process of setting and communicating boundaries effectively, fostering relationships based on mutual respect and understanding.

In addition, we explore the diverse forms of relationships that contribute to our lives—friendships, romantic partnerships, familial connections, and community ties. We offer guidance on nurturing and cultivating these different relationships, recognizing that each holds its own unique value and purpose.

Throughout this chapter, we provide practical exercises, reflection prompts, and actionable steps to help you create and nurture meaningful relationships. From building empathy and practicing forgiveness to engaging in acts of kindness and fostering shared experiences, we empower you to cultivate connections that bring joy, support, and fulfillment.

Remember, meaningful relationships require effort, time, and mutual investment. By prioritizing connection, fostering open-heartedness, and embracing the beauty of authentic relationships, you create a web of support and love that nourishes your soul and enhances your overall well-being.

Chapter 10

Healing through Creativity
Expressing Your Inner Voice

In this chapter, we explore the profound healing power of creativity and how it can serve as a gateway to expressing our inner voice. We delve into the various forms of creative expression and discover how engaging in creative pursuits can promote self-discovery, emotional healing, and personal transformation.

We begin by recognizing that creativity is inherent in every individual, regardless of artistic talent or skill level. We explore different outlets of creativity, such as writing, painting, music, dance, and more. Through these mediums, we learn to access the depths of our emotions, thoughts, and experiences, allowing them to manifest in tangible and transformative ways.

Next, we delve into the therapeutic benefits of creative expression. We explore how engaging in creative activities can serve as a form of self-care, stress relief, and emotional release. By immersing ourselves in the creative process, we tap into our subconscious minds, accessing hidden insights and discovering new perspectives on our lives.

Furthermore, we discuss the role of creativity in self-discovery. Through artistic exploration, we gain a deeper understanding of our desires, passions, and values. We learn to listen to our intuition, allowing our creative expression to guide us on the path of self-discovery and personal growth.

In addition, we explore the concept of art as a means of storytelling. We discover how sharing our creative works can create connections with others, foster empathy, and inspire change. We encourage you to embrace vulnerability and share your creations, recognizing the power they hold in touching the hearts and minds of others.

Throughout this chapter, we provide practical exercises and prompts to ignite your creativity and support your healing journey. From journaling and free writing to engaging in visual art or movement, we offer tools to help you unlock your creative potential and tap into the healing energy of self-expression.

Remember, the creative process is a personal and unique experience. There are no right or wrong ways to be creative. By embracing your inner voice and allowing it to manifest through creative expression, you embark on a transformative journey of self-discovery, healing, and authentic self-expression.

Chapter 11

Reclaiming Joy
Finding Happiness Within

In this chapter, we explore the concept of joy and its significance in our lives. We delve into the practices, mindset shifts, and perspectives that allow us to reclaim joy and cultivate a sense of happiness from within.

We begin by examining the nature of joy and how it differs from temporary pleasures or external circumstances. We delve into the idea that joy is a state of being that arises from within, independent of external factors. By recognizing this inherent nature of joy, we free ourselves from the dependence on external validation or circumstances for our happiness.

Next, we explore the power of gratitude in cultivating joy. We dive into the practice of gratitude and its ability to shift our focus from what we lack to the abundance that surrounds us. Through gratitude, we develop an appreciation for the present moment and find joy in the simple pleasures of life.

Furthermore, we discuss the importance of self-care and self-compassion in nurturing joy. We explore the practices of self-care that replenish our energy, bring us peace, and allow us to prioritize our well-being. By cultivating self-compassion, we create a foundation of love and acceptance that nurtures our inner joy.

In addition, we delve into the idea of finding joy in the journey rather than solely focusing on the destination. We embrace the concept of mindfulness and being fully present in each moment, recognizing the beauty and joy that can be found in even the simplest of experiences.

Throughout this chapter, we provide practical exercises and strategies to help you reclaim joy in your life. From engaging in activities that bring you joy to practicing mindfulness and self-compassion, we offer tools to support your journey towards lasting happiness.

Remember, joy is an inherent aspect of your being. By shifting your mindset, cultivating gratitude, practicing self-care, and embracing the present moment, you reclaim your birthright to joy and create a life filled with authentic happiness.

Chapter 12

Embracing Change
Navigating Life's Transitions

In this chapter, we explore the inevitability of change and how to navigate life's transitions with grace and resilience. We delve into the various types of change we encounter—both expected and unexpected—and offer guidance on embracing change as an opportunity for growth and transformation.

We begin by acknowledging that change is a natural part of life. We explore the emotions and resistance that often arise in the face of change and provide strategies to navigate them effectively. By developing a mindset of acceptance and adaptability, we open ourselves up to the possibilities that change brings.

Next, we delve into the process of letting go and releasing attachments that no longer serve us. We explore the role of self-reflection in understanding our fears and resistance to change, allowing us to release them and embrace new beginnings. By letting go of what no longer aligns with our authentic selves, we create space for personal growth and positive transformation.

Furthermore, we discuss the importance of self-care during times of change. We explore the practices that support our well-being, such as maintaining healthy routines, seeking support from loved ones, and practicing self-compassion. By prioritizing self-care, we nurture our resilience and ability to adapt to the changes that life presents.

In addition, we explore the power of reframing and finding opportunities within change. We delve into the concept of growth mindset, where challenges and transitions are seen as catalysts for personal development and expansion. By reframing our perspectives, we can navigate change with a sense of optimism and possibility.

Throughout this chapter, we provide practical tools and exercises to help you navigate life's transitions. From journaling and reflection to visualization and goal setting, we offer guidance on embracing change and stepping into a future filled with new possibilities.

Remember, change is a constant in life. By embracing change as an opportunity for growth, cultivating resilience, and practicing self-care, you can navigate life's transitions with grace and discover the transformative potential that lies within each change.

Chapter 13

Cultivating Mindfulness
Living in the Present Moment

In this chapter, we delve into the practice of mindfulness and its transformative effects on our lives. We explore the art of living in the present moment, free from the distractions of the past and worries about the future. By cultivating mindfulness, we enhance our well-being, reduce stress, and deepen our connection to ourselves and the world around us.

We begin by defining mindfulness as the practice of bringing our attention to the present moment with non-judgmental awareness. We explore the benefits of mindfulness, such as increased focus, improved emotional regulation, and enhanced overall mental and physical well-being.

Next, we delve into the various techniques and practices that can help cultivate mindfulness in our daily lives. From mindfulness meditation to mindful movement and sensory awareness, we offer practical tools to anchor our awareness in the present moment. By engaging in these practices regularly, we train our minds to be more present and attuned to the richness of each moment.

Furthermore, we discuss the role of self-compassion in mindfulness. We explore the practice of treating ourselves with kindness, understanding, and acceptance, especially when our minds wander or we encounter difficulties in staying present. By cultivating self-compassion, we create a nurturing environment for our mindfulness practice to flourish.

In addition, we explore the integration of mindfulness in everyday activities, such as eating, walking, and interacting with others. We delve into the concept of "mindful living," where each moment becomes an opportunity for presence and connection. By bringing mindfulness into our daily routines, we infuse our lives with a sense of intentionality and appreciation.

Throughout this chapter, we provide guided mindfulness exercises and practical tips to help you cultivate mindfulness in your life. From breath awareness and body scans to mindful eating and loving-kindness meditation, we offer tools to support your journey towards living in the present moment.

Remember, mindfulness is a lifelong practice. By incorporating mindfulness into your daily life, you enhance your ability to be fully present, find peace within, and experience the beauty of each moment.

Chapter 14

Embracing Resilience in Relationships
Navigating Challenges Together

In this chapter, we explore the importance of resilience in relationships and how to navigate challenges, conflicts, and changes within the dynamics of our connections with others. We delve into the principles and practices that promote healthy, resilient relationships and offer guidance on building and maintaining strong bonds that withstand the test of time.

We begin by recognizing that all relationships encounter obstacles and face periods of difficulty. We explore the common challenges that arise in relationships, such as communication breakdowns, conflicts, and life transitions. By acknowledging these challenges, we set the stage for developing resilience and growth within our connections.

Next, we delve into effective communication as a cornerstone of resilient relationships. We explore the art of active listening, expressing emotions constructively, and fostering empathy and understanding. By cultivating healthy communication patterns, we create a foundation of trust, respect, and openness within our relationships.

Furthermore, we discuss the importance of conflict resolution and problem-solving skills in navigating challenges within relationships. We explore strategies for managing conflicts, such as practicing active problem-solving, seeking win-win solutions, and embracing compromise. By approaching conflicts with empathy and a willingness to understand different perspectives, we foster resilience and growth within our relationships.

In addition, we explore the role of support and connection in building resilient relationships. We delve into the power of emotional support, encouragement, and validation in nurturing the well-being of both individuals within the relationship. By cultivating a supportive environment, we create a safe space for vulnerability and growth.

Throughout this chapter, we provide practical exercises and tools to enhance resilience within relationships. From practicing effective communication and active listening to engaging in activities that promote connection and understanding, we offer guidance on building strong and resilient bonds.

Remember, resilient relationships require effort, commitment, and a willingness to embrace challenges as opportunities for growth. By cultivating resilience within our connections, we create nourishing and enduring relationships that enrich our lives.

Chapter 15

Embracing a Life of Meaning:
Living with Purpose and Impact

In this final chapter, we delve into the significance of living a life of meaning and purpose. We explore the power of aligning our actions with our values and passions, and how embracing a life of purpose brings fulfillment, joy, and a positive impact on the world around us.

We begin by delving into the process of self-reflection and introspection to uncover our core values, passions, and aspirations. By understanding ourselves at a deeper level, we gain clarity on what truly matters to us and what brings us a sense of purpose and fulfillment.

Next, we explore the concept of purposeful action and how to align our daily lives with our values and aspirations. We discuss the importance of setting meaningful goals, prioritizing our time and energy, and making choices that align with our purpose. By living in alignment with our values, we create a sense of congruence and fulfillment in our lives.

Furthermore, we delve into the power of service and making a positive impact on others and the world. We explore the various ways we can contribute to the well-being of others, such as acts of kindness, volunteering, or pursuing a career that serves a greater cause. By channeling our passions and talents into meaningful endeavors, we create a ripple effect of positive change.

In addition, we discuss the role of self-care and maintaining balance while pursuing a life of purpose. We explore strategies for managing our well-being, setting boundaries, and nurturing our physical, mental, and emotional health. By taking care of ourselves, we ensure that we have the energy and resilience to make a lasting impact.

Throughout this chapter, we provide practical exercises and reflection prompts to help you discover and embrace a life of meaning and purpose. From creating a personal mission statement to taking inspired action, we offer tools to guide you on your journey towards a purpose-driven life.

Remember, living with purpose and impact is a lifelong journey. By aligning your actions with your values, pursuing your passions, and making a positive difference in the world, you create a life of meaning and fulfillment.

Congratulations on reaching the final chapter of

"The Healing of Internal Self"! I hope this book has provided you with valuable insights and guidance on your journey of self-healing and personal growth.

www.ingramcontent.com/pod-product-compliance
Lightning Source LLC
Chambersburg PA
CBHW050013090426
42733CB00018B/2649